'mamaseko

'mamaseko

Thabile Makue

University of Nebraska Press / Lincoln

"and this is nose" previously appeared in *The Sol Plaatje European Union Poetry Anthology*, vol. 7, comp. Liesl Jobson (Auckland Park: Jacana, 2017); "and these are eyes," previously appeared in *20.35 Africa: An Anthology of Contemporary Poetry*, ed. Safia Elhillo and Gbenga Adesina (Madison WI: Brittle Paper, 2018), 29; "the wailers," "body over water," "end haunt," "giving birth to my mother," "grandmother's heart," "end year," and "the daughter's inheritance" previously appeared as an untitled lyric essay in *New Daughters of Africa: An International Anthology of Writing by Women of African Descent*, edited by Margaret Busby (London: Harper Collins, 2019), 780–86.

The African Poetry Book Series has been made possible through the generosity of philanthropists Laura and Robert F. X. Sillerman, whose contributions have facilitated the establishment and operation of the African Poetry Book Fund.

Library of Congress Cataloging-in-Publication Data
Names: Makue, Thabile, 1992– author.
Title: 'mamaseko / Thabile Makue.
Description: Lincoln: University of Nebraska Press, [2020] | Series: African poetry book series |
Identifiers: LCCN 2019030988
ISBN 9781496219602 (paperback: alk. paper)
ISBN 9781496220097 (epub)
ISBN 9781496220103 (mobi)
ISBN 9781496220110 (pdf)
Classification: LCC PR9369.4.M347
A6 2020 | DDC 821/.92—dc23
LC record available at https://lccn.loc.gov/2019030988

Set in Garamond Premier by Laura Ebbeka.

'mamaseko ore o seke oa tsutulla sefate o sa batle ho besa mollo
'mamaseko[1] says[2] (italicize[3]) *do not uproot a tree unless[4] to burn a fire*

---

1 mother of tradition so mother of lineage so mother of blood
2 in a floating language hanging off the roof of a daughter's mouth the way smoke rises
3 make-believe there is ownership of words in a language in transit
4 inaccurate translation

LI TAOLA

LI TEBOHO

for tlhonolofatso, 'mamaseko, motlagomang, matshidiso, tebogo, limakatso.

'mamaseko

mali

maseko

my mother's name
'mamaseko
mother of tradition
mother of blood
bearer of covenant
> *makes me blood*
> *makes me unbending*
> *makes me grief*
> *makes me black lace*
> > *around neck*
> *makes me repetition*

> *makes me aloe*
> *makes me burnt offering*
> *makes me incense*
> *makes me penance*
> *makes me doctrine*
> *makes me sacrament*
> *makes me a shaved head*

> *makes me a house*
> *makes me law*
> *makes me written*
> > *in blood*
> *makes me unwritten by fire*
> *makes me never infant*
> *makes me black night*
> *makes me a story narrated*
> > *by rocks standing to make true*
> *makes me heavy*

> *makes me heavy*
> *makes me heavy*

giving birth to my mother

to mother

to give beginning
to bring forth
in parturition

to be born

to be blood
to begin
not at the very beginning
to begin
at lineage
to begin
before you begin

to mother

to extract from yourself

to daughter

to become mother

in this way
i give birth to my mother
in the same way
that she is my mother

by extraction
by blood
by becoming

unborn

she tries to leave

her mother's womb

bares claws

inside

there are trees
in our house

swinging black
swinging blue

screaming
needing

trees
and names

will break your house
when too close

these
are for the neighbors

outside in the day
eating sour fruit

outside

my mother undresses
by accident
she pours herself out
and i catch her
with my mouth
down the desert hallway
in my throat
she finds a body
i borrowed once
by accident
i have my mother
in my lungs
my grandfather breaks
out of his torso
onto the floor
my grandmother trips
over him
she bleeds out
into my mother's ear
my mother has her mother
in her windpipe
a magician
she smokes herself
into a potion
my mother has drunk
in her nose
i am sorry i am hungover
my mother's body
is intoxicated
i stumble out in my sleep

and you tuck me back in
by accident
you undress me
and all the alone
falls out

the bondage

we are bound by our sadness
blood thickened by torment
ribs bending together for
or against agony
our rocks cling together
over the old country
and our loss is one color

the daughter's inheritance

my daughters
will come to know
the pain of the womb
which transcends
the blood cord
they will know
the melancholy
of breaking open
for another
to be

and they that be
shall forever
know the wailing
of extraction
and then
the emptying
longing
the endless
wanting
the moonless sky
pining
insatiable sadness
unmediated
by a day of love

my daughters
will come to know
the little deaths
of waiting

and waiting
of being unwanted
by everything

and their medicine
shall be the blood
of their bodies
broken over
decayed
rocks beneath
the water

her mother's loss

the accusing hand
of a sad daughter
points to her face
and there lies awake
the full amassing
of her mother's loss

the children's right

and the god is jealous
and the god shall punish

the children for
their parents' wickedness

for the prodigal womxn
daughters shall find

no love to cling to
for the wrath of the man

the daughter shall ache
and not be filled

and the grandfather's
stones shall land

on the back of a weeping
granddaughter

this is the law
of the lord

and forever shall daughters
reap the trauma

of their parents' cruelty
and neither shall water

quench nor wine soothe
the heart broken by god

giving birth to my father

you taste your father's
ejaculation from your mother's mouth
your children are born
feet first
with faces that twist and twitch
and mouths full
of so much poison
your nipples turn black
and everything you sow
grows smoke
talks the fire back to you

your mother let the dark man's tongue
draw gravesites over her body
now your womb cannot labor anything but ghosts
and every man you know is mist
your mother swallowed
the bad man's air
now your lungs are filled
with forests on fire
and all of your children are black
who magicians
turn to powder
before your eyes

you wash yourself in the aloe
and the bitter stays
all of your children
are stillborn
your mother let a rotten man

pee in her
now your body is sick
and all your children are maggots
who grow wings soon enough
and leave you

grandmother's womb

my grandmother suffered a mental problem
twice in a jealous fit she let the dogs out on her daughter
she said she had a wolf in her heart
eight times the wolf in her bed watched her ravage herself
the tenth time was a niece
noosed on a tree
four times castor bean in a cup
each time missed the boat
almost ran out of chest
but did not run the wild thing out of body

on the radio they said one daughter
but she never birthed the odd girl
never left crease on the hem or an outlying girl
a biological mishap
a swaying skirt
damp feet knock knees
jittery within vacuum
prancing on the crook
found hanging skew
from some thatch roof
my grandmother does not remember what girl this is
what face she is wearing
what snapped neck
what man found within
alleged to have trespassed
broken in
taken the silver
fractured the china
what husband
what cannibal ate this foggy faced girl

my grandmother insists
that she labored four feathered girls
lightweight legs for takeoff
bright wings
soft spoken like her mother
fourteen times she's heard the old footsteps
felt the flutter on her hairs
but not once has she seen this daughter
did not even smell the carcass
did not see the dangling bones
the buzzing beasts

she recalls the man
pulls him from out of her crotch
but nothing of the cold girl
my grandmother may
or may not have birthed a girl
and then hauled her back into her pussy
she has a mental problem
a heart problem
or a womb problem

she laid two eggs
hatched them both with a fork
and knife ready in hand
she remembers
vaguely
the girl who went
but not the one who stayed
remembers the man who scorned her
but not the scorn
my grandmother's daughter hangs elusive

blood crowing

a womxn with eight legs
torn larynx in between faces
red lipstick over a beak
tail in turquoise boots
in grandmother's kitchen
wax weeping off thatch
hits the dung
fuse rises
outside hens crowing
inside blood crowing
name swaggering
portrait
oil on canvas

uncreation

there will be no more echoing
no more dittoing
you will not be bridge
be noon
if the boys be morning
and the girls be eventide
you will not parrot
will not sound an entire sky
with your rickety mouth
though the riddle be your tongue
you will not say the others
when asked for your name
though looking glass be your ovaries
you will not be vantage point
cannot hold all the dialect
or the ruined place
you cannot be all the faces
of all the womxn
cannot be all the blood
by yourself
be no longer resemblance
lay to rest the haunt
and then sleep a full night

'mele

and these are eyes

through the lens   an infant beholds color

dew for mother   sunset fire and blood

is father   blue gray for distant escarpment

pink tongues are words   and swords

her skin is august   soil is home

wind carries brown   over the border

river is the border   sand is at home

sand is lost   loss is black

the infant is also black   cloud is god

to know is white foam   white foam over pink tongue

when grandmother dies   sun turns everything brown

makes everything home   land and skin

both without god   love is blood

love stains memory   love stains god

and dad is home   red white purple rainbow

makes infant black   makes infant foam

turns foam to dew   cloud too makes dew

sun unmakes dew   dew is not home

dew foams over pupil   and infant beholds the color of homelessness

and these are lips

sweet sour falls simpler into the mouth
remains behind the teeth

where only sweetness
may be remembered

may burrow cavity
may swallow you

from the inside
of your own mouth

may pour honey over
all the absences

may coat cinnamon over
all the abscesses

may grow too big
may throw you out

may replace all the things you know
with sugar

may make empty
sugar

lonely could rot your teeth
lost love may make you sick

these are lips
and these are names

and this is nose

sacrifice rises
fills the room
with frankincense
burnt womxn are offering
oil on canvas
sweet smoke from canvas
may suffocate a chest
may suffocate a sky
this is how you tell
mother and father apart
mother is perfume
mother is incense
mother is atonement
mother is litany
mother is prayer
prayer is also smog
father is paraffin
father exhales
and supplication
is a womxn's body
you can't empty him out
without starting a fire
you can't pray
without inhaling a fire
and how many years
could mother burn
before she is powder
and what can you inherit
from cremation
other than to kneel

at the breaking of a man's rib
or his toe
or a scratch on a wrist
and this is how you tell
mother from father
father sins
and mother is penance
father sighs
and mother is penance
father sings
and mother is penance

and this is tongue

and this is repetition

and these are ears

and this is quiet quiet

and this is heart

thumping blue black
    a thousand flutters
        none of them mine
you come
    and then you go
        far out of the mile
into a new moon
    and this heart
        turns blue
remains blue
    will not warm to touch
        will not soften to arms
will not begin
    a new day
        or a new face
or a hand holding
    for nothing but to hold
        and this is heart
and this is echoing
    blue blue blue

'mele oa bobeli

root body

i know the root
the house the mass
the body the bone
to barter with sea
the brown and penance
the digging and dung
the libation above
i know the root
the awe and quick abhorrence
the years beyond
the hands lunging
the aids the marrow
the stress the duty
and blame and breadth
knee and torso
the cleft and hunger
the birth and ruin
mother and abolition
i know the root
the children and trigger

year body

some of the years
happen without
the body
the childhood
is an empty bed
high school
a shadow of flesh
adulthood the silhouette
of a womxn
without a mouth
some nights
i am water
spread thin
spread beyond myself
and to love
is to try
and pool myself together
believe me
i do not make you dive
on purpose
i need to see
if you'll come out
on the other side
if there is another side
if this body
is something
to swim through
and emerge alive
tell me
did you see

the others at the bottom
were there any bodies
to attest to their visit
the night ends
and was it here
if nobody wakes
as proof
was there a night
if the body
was not there
to witness it
and what of the damage
was it there if the body
cannot remember
was the blood lost
if the body made it up
where have
the years gone
without their body
and what places
have i gone
without my body

blood body

there is
only one way
to stop the blood
and it is to starve
to stop a war
you hunger
three days
to cheat
your death
you deny
the body
for forty days
to quiet your body
you deprive it
for twenty one days
my grandmother
teaches me that prayer
is surer this way
it is not
that god listens better
when you are empty
it is that
your blood is banished
and with it
your body of pain
it is that
your blood is banished
and with it
the weight of the name
it is that

your blood is banished
and with it
your yen
i begin the prayer
of famine
at sixteen
and to lose
the blood
is to gain
the god
in the hospital
the tube of food
brings the blood
rushing back
and i am anguished
you understand
don't you
that i remain
hungry against the blood
that the hunger
is a body
full of fight
if not
of prayer
that to be full
is to be blood
and i am afraid
of the other side
beyond the
prayer walls
where the war has come
where the death has come
where the body has awoken

time body

the body's affliction
is always now
now when the day
is gone
now when the house
has eaten the children
now when the walls
are parched for the womxn
now when this body is
the womxn
when the womxn is tired
when there is a wolf
in her heart
and foxes out
her door
now when she is hungry
for everything
and when she is hungry
for herself
when she is black
and night and opaque
and mad
and taken from herself
her body is now
always now
when the memory
tells her to kneel
and cry now
now when trauma climbs
over her and says

abate little strong womxn
succumb to your breaking
body now
now when she cannot run
when help cannot come
and when help has arrived
and is the fox
she had to banish
her body is now
where she will rot
to be made free
where she will drink hemlock
to chase away the smell
the mean manhood
the hands tossing rocks
the eyes taking her
in awe
and the pity and regret
the body's suffering
is always now
now when the body
has finished itself

too many body

the body
is many
one day is
a new body
another is
a resurrection
the body reincarnated
from itself
a new one
within the old one
yesterday's body
behind today's
each named
after the one lost
the one you love
is replaced by one
you do not know
the one i climb into
has gone
and i am purged
by another
the broken one
is the carcass
of another
a visitor makes
a body
a kiss another
love awakens
the others
and the death

of one is the birth
of another
a body for my blood
two for the clot
another for my mother
the name is three
a body for each
one of those
lost to find
this country
another for
the old country
another for the border
another is the rain
a body marks
the beginning
of the new year
another remains
to remind us
of the old year
of the old contract
of the lost blood
the body is broken
in death
every man
eats a full one
to remember
each body atonement
each one prayer
the body is the son
is a father giving
what is not his
the cost of the body
is the betrayal of memory

this body is a door
swung open
at your touch
the body of endings
appears to close
the gates
the body is a serpent
all its heads
are bodies
one to love you softly
another to eat
your neck
the one that
sends you away
is the cleanser
comes to rid the others
of their mistakes
the other is a swallow
leaping into a new country
the nomad body
leaves before
another is awake
the lapse is a body
of sacrifice
to compensate
the body is a daughter
the other is a mother
another a sibling
another the crime
the other the law
and the justice
the fight body is
the flight body
and the one

that remains
is a terrified child
is a neurotic hand
scabbing at itself
making a body
of horror
a monument
for the sad ones
and the angry ones
the medicine body
is the end body
is the poison body
is the body of
completion
come to haul
all the bodies
back into itself
into the void
the end body
is the birth body
is the new year
is the memory
is the birth
is the tail of the snake
born before the head
the old country
to dig the ghost
of the new
the daughter
to give birth
to the mother
and another
and another

fight body

i don't know
how to explain
it
the gape
the body
full of bone
and marrow
and skin
hollow

you feel
this heat
almost to a boil
and a cold
to the bones
at once

i think
my body
tries to
leave itself
escape into
a wilderness
of swords
pressed to
a name
without its flesh

i tell them
to send

the dust
into the ocean
at dusk
sing a sad song
do not dance

i secretly
want the void
i try for it
a cup of gun
beyond the torso
but i remember
too much

i say
send me
the sharp edge
no more puncture
i want the explosion
and body
entirely broken
beyond patch up

i don't know
much for this fear
that sends
me to the barrel
of the gun
i know that my mother
married hers
my grandmother too
and maybe
there is no way
to put it out

without going
into it

i guess this is
the work
of torture
to free
at last
a body from
its useless armor
to fall
into the fall
and say
it is at will

i don't know
if it's any true
but i ate the blood
that haunts me
to form alliance
with the knife
at my side
this way
it's not betrayal
just a fracture
at the rib
and i hope
the whole thing
catches the flame

wound body

in full bloom
the injury
has become
the body

naha

not to die alone

oh home
you four legged beast
you breathless tree
you spinning spider
you darting fuckgirl
you will not yield to me
you will not come to me
while i am awake
oh unlock me
fuck me if you must
and i might come to you
yield to your chasm
rest in your open field
if you say forever mine
or just for the night
i will do it for a half glance
for a moonless sky
at ten cents a minute
for a quarter pillow
to lie my head
a barely lit chest
scuffling underneath
a song about a place
a quick passing year
short despair
small small torture
just to taste my name
on the lips of another
even if it's only to fall off

quick passing
a year of a million short despairs
many many little tortures
oh home
won't you call for me just this once

refugee bones

battle breaks out over my mother's body
a blood bath spilling over
marking everything
she seeks asylum in a man
sets up camp over his chest
with a daughter on her back
i do not have a home
my country is a rotting man

mantsoe

literate   to know which words to use

eloquent   to know how to use the words

articulate   to say the thing you mean

illiterate   to not know the words to use
> to call yourself
> to call your children
> to call your body
> to call a country
> to call this country
> to call home to you

ineloquent   to not know how to use words
not from here
> to name things
from here
> to name yourself
> to name your children
> to name a country
> to name this country
> to name a place
> or a person
> or a song
> home

inarticulate   to have only the wrong language
to name yourself with
to give your children names

that cannot be manifested
where they are not heard
to name a country after a place
to name this country a place
to call a lover the wrong name
to call yourself the wrong name

before the next one

rainbow after the storm
rainbow before the next storm
before you wake up here again
your triggers beckon you
back into the stomach of a shark
the floor is the trigger
your body is the shark
your skin bellows
a rainbow pours out
and they applaud
what beauty
when you hurt
who could save you
from all that color

out of battle

a word summons us from sand
places boats where rivers were borders
oceans turn into trains
hours are trees
waiting is waking
continents are country
in summertime
love makes you a city
dressed in pink clouds
this is geography
your body is honey
poured over all the lines

secheso

passage

at midnight
levitation
a fourteen-legged bird crawls
over the stomach of an atlas
slithers in through liquid hole
toddler
granddaughter
arrives on the back of old womxn
grandmother
at a church
mosebetsi in the backyard
brown girl nailed to a raft
six packs of craft beer
on a wheelbarrow
paraffin down the throat of brown girl
earlier that week
toddler
granddaughter
finds a purse filled with fourteen bottles of perfume
old womxn
grandmother
bathes her in the sweet incense
and then burning raft
toddler
granddaughter
when in the flame
is just brown girl
familiar

mollo

those who live
by the spear
will die
by the spear

which is to say
those who die
by the water
had lived

for the same
knee deep
running against
the current

marriage distress signal

marry an ocean
arrive on a mud boat
heavy
      sinking
labor a girl
for balance
paddle into the tide
      capsize
and then set the girl
on fire
for help

church womxn

she lets the wind in
that night she learns
the wide of oceans
and the sinking in of bodies
under the moonlight
she mistakes potion for medicine
she falls head-first into it
reaches out to body
body turns to water
she does not cry help
cannot accept that she called the sea home
and opened her mouth while it swallowed her
did not let it out before drowning
did not swim to breath
is many knee bent womxn
swallowing gas
chocking
refusing to burp

the wailers

our womxn
are known for their cry
and knee bent wailing
impepho floating above them
from them
our men
look for girls
with large mouths
and husk over their
voices
and their tongues
split
between countries
of men
who are fathers
and men
who are trees
and their daughters are planted
by the rotting
and they are starved
until they know how to plead
how to lie on their stomachs
and cry
until they are ours

hush now baby

silence begets the girl
or a sink hole churns
in the womxn's womb
and a girl is born
in flight mode
with a tongue in throat
and dead air in the eyes
unmoving and opaque
scolding men
with her audacity for stillness
not voicelessness
quiet current
a numbness you must consent to
one you must knuckle under
at will
an omission of defense
refusal to war
to acknowledge
the violence of his presence
this is how to give birth
the girl is born for the sake of silence
or silence is born for the girl
this is how to make love
men must run
someone should tell them
that a quiet tide
swallows you all the same
the girl will not say no
the girl will not say anything

close

our curse is broken
the rib is back to the lender
our faces are no longer fast
our bodies no more feast
no more lodging
our hands not alms
our silences stark
no longer full of no
or i said no
our names not waiting
no longer treaty
no longer sweet
where be sour sour
our faces no more intimation
no longer silhouettes
of men who never came
we are no longer haunt
the curse is broken
we spilled blood
out of our own vaginas
and drank it
until we had forgiven
our offspring will be born
first with faces
to be seen before
they are sexed
and if they forget themselves
they will be blood offering
to appease the gods
a promise to slaughter

reappearances of our fathers
to eight generations
our curse shall be broken
at the birth of children
who will name themselves

the handmaid's psalm

after the handmaid's tale

give me children
or else i die
make me branches
over my country
let my seed be
fervent crop
over my mother's land
water my daughters
with the blood of their fathers
let the soil be holy
dung be the men's bones
a quarter pound
of fermented semen
be the water over their leaves
observe the seventh day
call it the year of pollination
and my daughters
shall swell with fruit
and the earth shall be theirs
for their fight
and their riot shall bear harvest
and the heavens
shall come upon them
and their rivers shall be full

give me daughters
lest i die
make them branches
over the old country

popelo

gray mountain

my grandmother is
a mountain
standing guard
for her children
gray green brown black
habitually distant

sunset

the children gathered around
to watch in awe
the remarkable departure

sunrise

to wake is unremarkable
habitual and perfunctory
and indeed they did not notice
their dawn come
and its joy was dew
not to quench the famish
but to pass by the lip
to mock the tongue
and to disappear

moonlight

it was the moon
that taught them
to shape shift
on the faces of their men
to shine without
all their light
to be half full
and to swallow the sky

starlet

they burned together
like the stars
dead blood sprouting
across the great dark sky

to be wind

you could say
the wind taught them
the lines
or maybe the wind drew
the rivers
and mountains
and dogs
and people
in between
countries
maybe the wind
made them
the lines

river border bosoms

the river taught them
to be brown
to be thick
and full of water
to be still
to run
in
between countries
and people

the purge i

they were mud houses
during the year of the rain
wilting purging

drought

and the drought
taught them to starve

the flood

a cup too full
will drown
your children

the purge ii

they purge in menopause
a bit of their fire
and in hail
a bit of their cold

bolokoe

peppermint girl

she lay sprawled out in the dirt
maybe sand again
in the kitchen
watermint or spearmint
bubbling in a hot kettle
peppermint
a hybrid herb at boiling point
at the will of a man at boiling point
hybrid lover and knife
her
hybrid womxn
flight risk
turns herself in occasionally
garden girl
herbs in the backyard girl
body discovered in the backyard girl
peppermint now gas
unclogging the kitchen
degreasing the man
now prickly
now one thing
now shinning sickle
one girl in body bag ma
once two things man
now bubbling in hot
peppermint scented kitchen
skin detoxed
but womxn is not the blockage

whole house still smell like her
hybrid girl
holy incense
man down girl
postmortem says smoke inhalation

hungry belly universe

the world is
a groaning belly
helpless desperate for us
annihilates us perhaps
for our own god
a sweet sickle
on our bare necks
each an unknowing
field of kernel
ahead of reap
a newly slaughtered
lamb dubious about death
chicken with miles
to cover before a boiling
pit of hot oil
the world is a mouth
my dear
full of hunger
and need
it will eat you
if you get lost
but it will eat you
if you stand fixed

those hungry girls

look at all
those hungry girls
so gorgeous
their crooked mouths
of famish and cackle
what beauty their bone
breaking through
to be witnessed
their tense hair
like new tinsel
their hard hands
and dark knees
like a loose girdle
see their eyes
of sorcerous starvation
it's unladylike isn't it
to be so clearly needing

pheko

ghost

hiroshima draws her first breath as a ghost
no one has forgotten how a city on fire engulfs itself

she says *you can come with me*
through the night you watch her thunder
the way hatsotelo womxn keep their husbands
under their tongues until their mouths are ghost towns
under her breasts
a country has split itself
she is a half mountain broken in war and in love
haunted by everyone she let stay
who died in the fire burned by the ones who left
you wonder if you're safe
remember that she did not say *come home with me*

remember that a city on fire leaves nothing to rescue

she says *you can get away with me*
you sleepover in a nomad city
by morning you're smoke suspended in the sky
and her kisses dizzy you
off your feet
loving her is swimming
and running
and hiding
and gasping
your love is fuel
your home is a city on fire
in her eyes the ocean spans wider
her i love you sounds like distance

like the other side of the world like not here to stay
like city under construction
her body is an hourglass running out of night time
do not move here if you're not sand
or suicidal

not to forget

if the ocean should rise   in the night

and cover us in salt   in breadth in never ending in near ending

should you go under   i will not find you again

if water should come   between us a sea of cold of old things of stale

if an iceberg should stand   between us to quake our hearts out of their torsos

if the tide should pull you   from me i cannot regain you

i think we have already lost   all our blood in the ocean

if time or aging   carries you away

i might be the ocean   and swallow all your body

and keep you   for myself

after all time has passed   slowly as if unmoving

the days toiling   the nights crawling

if you should go   slow into the night

and stay   then i might be the night

and keep you   in the darkest blue

grandmother's marriage

you were married to him for 65 years   *that's a long time*
sometimes love is a crowded place
a swelled stomach
water in the lungs
a dam and algae
a room waiting to put both of its arms around you
to gather all its walls around you
above you
to consume you in a kiss
to still your breath in a kiss
to unname you in a kiss
to rename you in a kiss

did you love him
sometimes love is an orchestra
after the show
backstage
preparing to get out of performance
but not yet done
still dressed in applause
in well done
more more i want you

was he kind
sometimes love is a house
living in your ducts
even after you've left it
an old pieture in circular motion
repeating itself
rehashing itself

a heart holding a past
a mind recreating a past

were you kind
sometimes love is a jealous god
a solitude that will not share you
a crowded place
a mall or a morgue
a mortician with his mouth over yours
until you have no breath of your own

to torch

people like you
will always find

people like me
it's science

maybe blood
how rubble collects

how ditches pile up
how we come together

it's religious
to flock together

to bind by the knee
two of the same

i love you
until my nose bleeds

i love you
for the breaking

into the stretched winter
for the ugly

people like me
will always find

people like you
it is hereditary to seek out our torture

apology to sara

dear sara
grandmother says that we were
born with war in our mouths

dear sara
war is not a sweet disposition
i miss you

how i missed the train over my body
the day i packed up all of my things
and headed to the tracks

when i didn't jump
i miss you like i almost fell
i almost broke my neck

i broke my heart
but hearts can be fixed

dear sara
i always thought of love as suicide
with you it was a homicide

now i have all this fight left in me
but you're not here

dear sara
i think i ate the shadows
i wanted to see you

so i ate the dark to clear up the air
i cannot live without you
is not the same thing
as i love you

the patch up

did you build her with rocks
did you split your hands
mixing tar
did you rapture bone
lose marrow
holding thatch
did it hurt a lot
was it heavy
to carry her all these years
did you pull flesh
from your torso
to complete her
is she full now
are you full now
did you forget the lull
did you fix her
until you had healed
all your neediness
did your father return
and pull you out
of her collapse
did you tell her
you were holding her
when you had fallen into
did you find the cure
did you love her
until your emptiness
was finished
did you drink from
her brim
are you whole now

the rot the peace

i wave the flag
first before the fight
puss pressed on
the window i say
look this ugly
this perfect infection
see its stinging thrust
punish me no longer
give me water and the serpent
and i will return to you
its head its tail
give me the slaughter
of your mother's flock
and i will give you
a pint of blood
from my own side
fight me no more
wave your gangrene
at the gate
let me see your ugly
and i will eat all our fight

where does love go

off into the year
months mold a new face
the water takes you into an endless sky
decades above sea level
into the gaping vastness
where all the unsaid things say themselves
and i want to touch you
in the way of old
but distance is a parasite
steals from memory
pulls you from my desperate hand
makes you
a song about leaving
i know all the words to it
and none of them are yours
my love is boarding a plane
in constant departure
all the hellos are goodbye
and i have forgotten how to see you
couldn't call you from a moving train
or one that had stopped

the hunger

the famine clutches
on

adorn your ribs
and they shift shape

into open shells
and i want to ask

you
to stay a bit

give me mouth
to mouth

before you go
give me a little limb

for the limp
give me a little lamp

for this dark blue
give me a little tongue

for the famish
hey   can you hear me

not to love you

i will not love you
midnight girl

i will not be stuck there
in between your pant and exhale

in that satiny groggy nook
to know everything that happened

before it happens
to patch up the hour after you have gone

before you come
at first

a sweet mouth
the face of a friend

or at least
hands not yet criminal

not yet tired
of begging the ghosts to go

of begging the girl to stay
in the room

in her body
and then

in an instant
or a whiff of a year

wrinkles everywhere
dandelion in a mouth

for good health with sea salt
to neutralize from shock

anti acid for almost holding
the face of an ex lover

a stranger related to a song
a street sign

hands in the act
begging nostalgia to go

moonlight back behind the hours
before they happen

i will not love you moon
i will not be found there

in between your inhale and sigh
in that slippery dizzy part

where it might be hard to tell
gathering clouds from those that have rained

baleful heart

to forget you
i ask for an
ocean between
our bodies
i ask for thunder
to preoccupy me
in a different dance
i ask salt
over the loss
i ask the memory
of your departure
to remain
and haunt me
if i start to sweeten
your name
i ask the night
to stay in your stead
i immerse my body
in water
tell it
that all drowning
does not kill you
and there are
near deaths
i can bring myself
and i don't have to
fuck each of them
to forget you
i drink honey
from the store

and i think maybe
it's just as sweet
without a sting
to the skin
or a needle
to the heart

phupjane

april

off white
and then fast blue gray
and then long lasting
deep blue

when april begins
deep blue settles
in the marrow
settles in the mirror

heckling blacks
could bring you here
in the springs of a mattress
wove you into the bedspread

and you can't keep it down
if it wants to leave you
you can't keep your wind down
if it's leaving

didn't you know
you couldn't keep a person
if they were wind
splitting rocks inside your gut

wanting to leave
you can't grip at the calves
or run after
in may

deep blue poised over you
couldn't let you race the corner
unless the brim
won't let you beg

with your mouth
unless cow dung over your feet
and a pinched toe
you'll sleep over the sky

off white
and then fast blue gray
and then just blue
and then eight aprils

phato

august[1] village
hut in the girl's stomach
inside
wolf
named father
howls through girl's mouth
howls through girl's hands
howls through girl's eyes
girl sent out of village
arrives in another
wearing the corpse
of old village
of the burning house
of the burning tree
says i love you
flings hut open
presses wolf into the mouth
of a lover
lets lover sleep there
over the chest
of a begging village
august girl
village in the hut
inside

---

1   august
    in a sepia village
    in a mud hut
    in the mouth of a wolf

113

the girl cannot find sleep
tosses burning house
turns burning tree
over its stomach
lets lover stay over
but
cannot stop the door howling
cannot stop the ground howling
cannot stop the windows howling

may wrists

what are wrists
during the long may night
frightening as shadows
when you stare
too long
a long mile
walking behind my mother
and what is breath
a ghost

and could you mourn it

wait

you wait out
on the grass
listen to the harmonica
of grass climbing
into you
your collarbone
whimpering blue blue
and waiting and waiting
and wanting
for passage
for quick blizzard
worming in and out
until completely out
and wait and wait
on a familiar mouth
wait to be swallowed
raked into
waiting and
imagining a person
into a body
walking forth
wait wait
tomorrow they arrive
and wait and wait
if tomorrow come

end ballade

cue the swan song
a book has closed
before another began

island be the story
sand surround this body
away from the salt

rattle it no longer
wake me no longer
the bell has sung

we are done now
let the doves out
we will be buried

on a winter's day
full of snow
cold cold

we will not cry
we will not fight
just lie still

float above ourselves
the onlookers will
sing a sad song

rain may pour
wind may come
and down down

you will go
and down down
you will remain

roof top blue

i look at a world
spread across
my ceiling
clung to my blankets
loosely sticky
against tempered skin
and i wonder
if we will ever say
once we were tired
and now we are alive
breathing
from inside the rib cage
we grew old
but did not grow dead
we waited
and the prize
of patience was glorious
we cried all our tears
that year
and then baptism came
and we grieved no more

will we heal at the knee
wake upright
did we slither through
this big world
on our stomachs
did we run the way up
its mountains
the heaps of mouths

and hands
and feet
did we make it alright
are we done now
are we dead now

end haunt

the haunt
that came
upon us
will not go
unless we
go with it

body over water

a body split
between countries
is a ship
standing
to be wrecked
the doors open
into landmines
and ghosts of
our fathers
and of girls
who came
and never left
who stayed
for the sad music
requiem for the womxn
who broke open
to labor children
psalm for the children
whose feet remained
in the womb
who toss and kick
but never begin
the treasures of
witchcraft venomoid
rusted under the clutter
of histories and recollections
dust settling deeper
into this day
and the doors creaking
open into daggers

into rope
into gas
into hemlock
into bullet
into ocean at night
calling the body
into itself
at the break of dawn
encircled by an army
of icebergs of lovers
and icebergs of friends
breaking in four parts
and then falling into
and remaining in
engines dead
the ghosts hidden under
the rubble
and the rubble
buried under itself

end year

in the year of healing
antihistamine shall
be a mirror
turned toward the heart
and the rot shall
be cached no longer
and the finger
pointed inward shall
pull out the dirt
of old
and the leaving
of trauma will hurt
like any feet
turned against
the pain will flush
through you
and another death
shall take your father
and another country
shall steal your mother's
softness
and another night shall
begin and remain a year
and another ballot shall come
and you will not be the choice
the puss pressed out
shall be the memory
of a lover who could
only stay in your heart
the anesthesia shall

leave by the second loss
of a name of a face
and the completion
shall be a room
with all your sadnesses
and the sun rushing in

LI TEBOHO

With deep gratitude to the universe. The gods. And for their vessel, my mother, 'Mamaseko, and isithunya who came before her.

For my sister, Tlhonolofatso Phakeli.

For Sarah Dlamini and Matshidiso Ntlhe.

My friends, Limakatso Sehaole, Tebogo Ramagaga, who listen with tireless empathy. Thandokuhle Mngcibisa and Vuyelwa Maluleke, who edit masterfully. Rejoyce Makhetha, Sibongile Zwane, Alulutho Mbendeni, Faith Kinniar, Koleka Putuma, Sinenhlanhla Mdiya, Roché Kester, Dani Alheit.

The African Poetry Book Fund and its board. Kwame Dawes for delivering the best news of my writing career, and for his brilliant editing. The University of Nebraska Press staff, for all the hard work to make a precious book of my manuscript.

And, late Patricia Miswa for giving me my first writing job.

li taola	warnings
mali	blood
maseko	traditions (also covenants)
'mele	body
'mele oa bobeli	second body
naha	coutry (also land)
mantsoe	words
secheso	sacrifice (also burnt offering)
mosebetsi	ritual (also work)
mollo	fire
popelo	womb
bolokoe	cow dung
pheko	medicine
phupjane	june
phato	august

IN THE AFRICAN POETRY BOOK SERIES

Your Body Is War
Mahtem Shiferraw

In a Language That You Know
Len Verwey

Logotherapy
Mukoma Wa Ngugi

When the Wanderers Come Home
Patricia Jabbeh Wesley

*Seven New Generation African
Poets: A Chapbook Box Set*
Edited by Kwame Dawes
and Chris Abani
(Slapering Hol)

*Eight New-Generation African
Poets: A Chapbook Box Set*
Edited by Kwame Dawes
and Chris Abani
(Akashic Books)

*New-Generation African Poets:
A Chapbook Box Set (Tatu)*
Edited by Kwame Dawes
and Chris Abani
(Akashic Books)

*New-Generation African Poets:
A Chapbook Box Set (Nne)*
Edited by Kwame Dawes
and Chris Abani
(Akashic Books)

*New-Generation African Poets:
A Chapbook Box Set (Tano)*
Edited by Kwame Dawes
and Chris Abani
(Akashic Books)

To order or obtain more information on these or other University of
Nebraska Press titles, visit nebraskapress.unl.edu. For more information
about the African Poetry Book Series, visit africanpoetrybf.unl.edu.

CPSIA information can be obtained
at www.ICGtesting.com
Printed in the USA
LVHW012301170120
644022LV00002B/303